H   Hope

O   Overcomes

P   Perseveres

E   Endures

By
John C Burt

FOREWORD :

This book is concerned with the whole concept of ' hope ' and what it means to have it. As a teaching method the letters of the word ' hope ' will be used to discuss various aspects of it. Hope, Overcomes, Perseveres and Endures. Each of these four will be discussed at some length during the discussions of this book.

My reason behind writing a book on such a thing as ' hope ' is that, in our days and times ,sometimes its in short supply. That is also including in the Christian Churches, which should be places where real ' hope ' resides on this planet earth. I want to attempt to generate greater levels of ' hope ' in you. This is particularly true, if you are in fact a Christian person. We should have " hope '; because we have a profound ' hope ' for the future in the second coming of Jesus Christ. At times even the Church can lose sight of this ' hope ' and at times does not hold to it too well. Jesus Christ is coming back to this planet earth and therefore we of all people on it should be incredibly full of ' hope ' particularly for the future with Him.

H Hope

Initially, I will be giving you a number of verses to do with the concept of ' hope ' from the Word of God. The version of the Word I am choosing to use for this exercise on the word ' hope ' is the Common English Bible. I believe its a fairly reasonable and even understandable translation of the Word of God.

{ CEB }

Psalm 33 : 20

(20) " We put our hope in the LORD.
        He is our help and shield."

Psalm 42 : 5

(5) " Why, I ask myself,
      are you so depressed?
      Why are you so upset inside?
       Hope in God !
      Because I will again give him
thanks,
       my saving presence and my God."

Psalm 62 : 5

(5) " Oh, I must find rest in God only

because my hope comes from him ! "

Psalm 130 : 5

  (5) " I hope LORD,
       My whole being hopes,
       and I wait for God's promise."

Psalm 146 : 5

  (5) " The person whose help is the God
of Jacob -
       the person whose hope rests in the
LORD their God -
       is truly happy ! "

Proverbs 13 : 12

(12) " Hope delayed makes the heart sick;

        longing fulfilled is a tree of life."

Proverbs 23 : 17 - 18.

(17) " Don't let your heart envy sinners,

        but fear the LORD constantly;

(18) then you will have a future,

        and your hope won't be cut off."

Isaiah 40 : 30 - 31.

(30) " Youths will become tired and weary,

        young men will certainly stumble;

(31) but those who hope in the LORD will renew their strength; they will fly up on wings like eagles; they will run and not be tired; they will walk and not be weary."

Jeremiah 29 : 11

(11) " I know the plans I have in mind for you, declares the LORD; they are plans for peace, not disaster, to give you a future filled with hope."

Romans 5 : 4 - 5.

(4) " endurance produces character, and character produces hope.

(5) This hope doesn't put us to shame,

because the love of God has been poured out in our hearts through the Holy Spirit, who has been given to us."

Romans 8 : 20 - 21.

(20) " Creation was subjected to frustration, not by its own choice - it was the choice of the one who subjected it - but in the hope

(21) that the creation itself will be set free from slavery to decay and brought into the glorious freedom of God's children. "

Romans 12 : 12

(12) " Be happy in your hope, stand your ground when you're in trouble, and devote

yourselves to prayer."

Romans 15 : 4

(4) " Whatever was written in the past was written for our instruction so that we could have hope through endurance and through the encouragement of the scriptures."

Romans 15 : 13

(13) " May the God of hope fill you with all joy an peace in faith so that you overflow with hope by the power of the Holy Spirit."

1 Corinthians 13 : 13

(13) " Now faith, hope, and love remain these three things - and the greatest of these is love."

1 Corinthians 15 : 19

(19) " If we have a hope in Christ only in this life, then we deserve to be pitied more than anyone else."

Colossians 1 : 27

(27) " God wanted to make the glorious riches of this secret plan known among the Gentiles, which is Christ living in you, the hope of glory."

1 Timothy 4 : 10

(10) " We work and struggle for this : " Our hope is set on the living God, who is the savior of all people, especially those who believe."

Hebrews 6 : 19

(19) " This hope, which is a safe and secure anchor for our whole being, enters the sanctuary behind the curtain."

Hebrews 10 : 23

(23) " Let's hold on to the confession of our hope without wavering, because the one who made the promises is reliable."

Hebrews 11 : 1

(1) " Faith is the reality of what we hope for, the proof of what we don't see."

1 John 3 : 3

(3) " And everyone who has this hope in him purifies himself even as he is pure."

Hope

From the outset and particularly after having taken time to read and think about the use of the word ' hope ' in the Word of God. One can see the important thing to deal with is what you actually put your ' hope ' in. From the Old Testament verses it can be seen that their ' hope ' was in the LORD God - Yahweh. Then in the New Testament we have Jesus Christ as the Son of God being the ' One ' people put their ' hopes ' and ' hope ' on. So in the end it really does matter what your ' hope ' is placed in and upon.

When we put our ' hope ' and ' hopes ' onto God we are not disappointed and are actually putting them into the ' One " we can really trust and believe in. In some ways its not very acceptable to both ' trust ' in God and also to have a ' hope ' in Him. Or may be I should have said its not fashionable to do both. At times in our day and age its like people believe that they have out - grown their need for both God and a ' hope ' in Him.

The Christian Church should when its working at its best ' be a beacon of hope in a dark and sometimes scary and fearful place for many people.' The place I am talking about is the world we all live in. Sometimes the world we all live in is a place where people trade in fear and darkness and even just plain evil. The Christian Church is I believe called to the ' beacon of hope ' in the midst of all of this in this world. Which in the end is why I believe that the Christian Church should be, and even needs to be one of the most ' hope - filled places ' on the planet earth. Yet sadly as I move around and observe and interact with Christians and Churches I find the opposite to be true. We as Christians have ' the hope of glory ' residing within us and therefore should be filled with ' hope '. We all have been taught about the second coming of Jesus Christ and we nod our heads in agreement that we believe He is coming back. However all too often that ' hope of glory ' and the return of Jesus Christ has not moved from our heads to our hearts and faces. My question to you is why are we not the people and ' beacons of hope ' we should be?

There is a whole world waiting expectantly for ' hope ' to come and we as the Christian Church have the Gospel which is the means and instrument of ' a real hope ' coming from God Himself. The ' hope ' of the Gospel is that we when we believe and accept Jesus Christ are given a way Back to God the Father. To me that is

' real hope ' and not the ' manufactured hope versions ' we are so often offered by many in this world. There are many who want to find both a way to God and a way of being at peace with Him as well. As carriers of the Gospel message we have both and therefore really should be ' beacons of hope ' to everyone around us in our communities.

To change tack for a minute; Hebrews 6 : 19 ' This hope, which is a safe and secure anchor for our whole being, enters the sanctuary behind the curtain.' ' This hope '; this ' hope ' is of course ' hope ' that comes through the finished work of Jesus Christ upon the Cross of Calvary. The point is that it is this ' hope ' in His finished work upon the Cross that gives us a ' hope' that is a safe and secure anchor for our whole being. Today there is a lot of talk about being anchored in your own life and belief. Yet we as Christians have a ' hope ' which is a safe and secure anchor for our whole beings already in our ' hope ' in and through Jesus Christ. Also, its an anchor for the whole of a person's being, a rock - solid foundation that they can and should build their lives upon.

Finally in relation to the word ' hope ' consider Hebrews 10 : 23, ' Let's hold on to the confession of our hope without wavering, because the one who made the promises is reliable."

Its not just enough to have a ' hope ' in Jesus Christ and His finished work upon the Cross; we also need to hold to that ' hope ' unwaveringly. The reason given by this verse is because the one who our ' hope ' is in and who has made promises is reliable. We can have an unwavering ' hope ' in Jesus Christ because simply we can and should trust Him to be the truth . He is also reliable and trustworthy. You cannot have a ' hope ' in somebody or something that is not reliable or even trustworthy.

O Overcomes

The translation of the Word used for the next three words will be the Hebrew - Greek Study Bible NIV.

Matthew 16 : 18

(18) And I tell you that you are Peter, and on this rock I will build my church, and the gates of Hades will not overcome it."

Mark 9 : 24

(24) " Immediately the boy's father exclaimed, " I do believe; help me overcome my unbelief."

Luke 10 : 19

(19) " I have given you authority to trample on snakes and scorpions and to overcome all the power of the enemy; nothing will harm you."

John 16 : 33

(33) " I have told you these things, so that in me you may have peace. In this world you will have trouble. But take heart ! I have overcome the world."

Romans 12 : 21

(21) " Do not be overcome by evil, but overcome evil with good."

1 John 2 : 13

(13) " I write to you fathers, because you have known him who is from the beginning.

I write to you, young men, because you have overcome the evil one.

I write to you, dear children, because you have known the Father."

1 John 4 : 4

(4) " You, dear children, are from God and have overcome them, because the one who is in you is greater than the one who is in the world."

1 John 5 : 4 - 5.

(4) " for everyone born of God
overcomes the world. This is the
victory that has overcome the world,
even our faith.

(5) Who is it that overcomes the
world? Only he who believes that
Jesus is the Son of God."

Revelation 2 : 7

(7) " He who has an ear, let him hear
what the Spirit says to the churches.
To him who overcomes, I will give the
right to eat from the tree of life, which
is in the paradise of God."

Revelation 2 : 26

(26) " To him who overcomes and does my will to the end, I will give authority over the nations."

Revelation 3 : 21

(21) " To him who overcomes, I will give the right to sit with me on my throne, just as I overcame and sat down with my Father on his throne."

Revelation 21 : 7

(7) " He who overcomes will inherit all this, and I will his God and he will be my son."

Overcomes

The next word to consider is that of ' overcomes '. I believe that the three words of overcomes, perseveres and endures come out of our sense of ' hope '. In the end result they are all really intimately caught up with ' hope ' and all its ramifications in and through our lives.

I believe our ability to overcome comes out of our real sense of ' hope '. Even the ' hope of glory ' and how real it is for us. Our ability to overcome also, depends on how much our sense of ' hope ' has invaded all the individual parts of our lives. The word overcomes in the New Testament is used in the sense of overcoming the world just as Jesus Christ overcame the world and prevailed over it. I would submit to even attempt to do this; one has to have and really needs a deep sense of the ' hope ' we have in Jesus Christ. To be able to overcome the world as He did will require us to really believe and adhere to the ' hope ' and the ' hope of glory ' we have in Jesus Christ.

There is also a prevailing sense in the New Testament of our need to overcome ' evil ' and ' Satan ' and his devices and ways and wiles. 1 John states that its young men who overcome ' evil '. Yet , I would believe that it is not just they that have to do this specifically; as if they are special cases in this regard. Again, to overcome ' evil ' and Satan and his devices and ways and wiles is caught with our sense of ' hope '. Particularly our sense of ' hope ' and ' real hope ' in the power and authority of Jesus Christ. Both in His demonstrated power and authority as the Son of God. But also in the power and authority of His name when we invoke and declare it. This is particularly true when we come against ' evil ' and the devices and ways and wiles of Satan. One in the end to do all of this; needs to have a very real sense of ' hope ' and particularly the ' hope of glory ' in and through Jesus Christ, the Son of God.

In the Book of Revelation there is a sense of the one who overcomes through the ' hope ' in Jesus Christ receiving the crown of eternal life from Jesus Christ, the So of God. Which is all the more reason to both have a very real sense of ' hope ' and the ' hope of glory ' which manifests itself itself in overcoming both the world and evil and Satan. It is the one who overcomes, not just in the short - term but also in the long - term. Through out the whole of their lives as they run the race set before them by the Lord of Glory.

All of which should both encourage us all to overcome the world and Satan and his ways and wiles. But also to grab with both hands a very real sense of the ' hope ', the ' hope of glory ' in and through Jesus Christ. This is all part and parcel of our inheritance when we become believers in and through Jesus Christ, the Son of God.

My prayer for us all is that we both find the ' hope ', the ' hope of glory ' , in and through Jesus Christ. And yet also come to the point where through the application of this very real ' hope ', the ' hope of glory , to and through our lives. That we overcome both the world and evil and Satan. May we all run the race before us all regards the ' hope of glory ' and overcoming the world and evil and Satan and his ways and wiles.

P Perseveres

Romans 5 : 3 - 4

(3) " Not only so, but we also rejoice in our sufferings, because we know that suffering produces perseverance,

(4) perseverance, character; and character, hope. "

2 Corinthians 12 : 12

(12) " The things that mark an apostle - signs, wonders and miracles - were done among you with great perseverance."

2 Thessalonians 1 : 4

(4) " Therefore, among God's churches we boast about your perseverance and faith in all the persecutions and trials you are enduring."

2 Thessalonians 3 : 5

(5) " May the Lord direct your hearts into God's love and Christ's perseverance."

Hebrews 12 : 1

(1) " Therefore, since we are surrounded by such a great cloud of witnesses, let us throw off everything that hinders and the sin that so easily entangles, and let us run with perseverance the race marked out for

us."

James 1 : 3 - 4.

(3) " because you know that the testing of your faith develops perseverance.

(4) Perseverance must finish its work so that you may be mature and complete, not lacking anything."

James 1 : 12

(12) " Blessed is the man who perseveres under trial, because when he has stood the test, he will receive the crown of life that God has promised to those who love him."

James 5 : 11

(11) " As you know , we consider blessed those who have persevered. You have heard of Job's perseverance and have seen what the Lord finally brought about."

2 Peter 1 : 5 - 6.

(5) " For this very reason, make every effort to add to your faith goodness; and to goodness, knowledge;

(6) and to knowledge, self - control; and to self - control, perseverance; and to perseverance, godliness;"

Revelation 2 : 2

(2) " I know your deeds, your hard work and your perseverance. I know that you cannot tolerate wicked men, that you have tested those who claim to be apostles but are not, and have found them false."

Revelation 2 : 19

(19) " I know your deeds, your love and faith, your service and perseverance, and that you are now doing more than you did at first."

{ Heb - GK Study Bible NIV }

Perseveres

From the outset in considering ' perseveres ', one has to note that its the object, person or cause one is preserving in, that's of prime importance. It's not just perseverance for the sake of perseverance, as if one was a strong person and could just preserve against all the odds.

Also, again I believe that ' hope', the ' hope of glory ' is something that can and does help us to persevere.

There used to be an advertising slogan; ' keeps on, keeping on.' This slogan from the world of advertising sums up for me how I view our need to preserve in the ' hope ', the ' hope of glory '. The reality is in the world of today there is a lot of persecution, slandering and just plain rumor - mongering regarding both the Christian Church and Christians individually. The Christian church and Christians have been marginalized and are on the outer of both the world and its cultures. Therefore, the crying need of both the Christian Church and Christians individually is to persevere in their ' hope', faith and belief in Jesus Christ and the ' hope of glory ' in Him and through Him.

One particular application of the word perseveres, that comes through again and again in the New Testament context. Is that of perseverance under trials or testing from the LORD God. The idea is that the LORD God will test our faith, belief an even our ' hope', the ' hope of glory ' , that we have. In the face of this there is a need to persevere, in the face of whatever comes or goes or happens in our lives. The ' hope ', the ' hope of glory', is the thing that can really help us persevere and to have perseverance, Even in the face of the time of trials, suffering, grief and or pain. Which is why the ' hope', the ' hope of glory ' is for us so important to both grasp and grab hold of. So that we can run the race before us. We can only do that in the power, authority and strength of the LORD God, Jesus Christ, the Son of God Himself.

The other thing that comes out of the verses from the Book of Revelation, is that, it delights the LORD God, Jesus Christ, the Son of God. Particularly when we evidence perseverance and persevere in our lives and its various trials and situations. In the Book of Revelation the Lord commends both the Churches individuals who have evidenced perseverance and persevered in their faith, hope and belief in and through Him. Which is all the more reason to continue and may well be even start to seek to add perseverance and persevering to your faith, belief and hope in Jesus Christ, the Son of God.

E Endures

Ecclesiastes 3 : 14

(14) " I know that everything God does will endure forever; nothing can be added to it and nothing taken from it. God does it so that men will revere him."

Malachi 3 : 2

(2) " But who can endure the day of his coming? Who can stand when he

appears? For he will be like a refiner's fire or a launderer's soap."

1 Corinthians 4 : 12 - 13.

(12) " We work hard with our own hands. When we are cursed, we bless; when we are persecuted, we endure it;

(13) when we are slandered, we answer kindly. up to this moment we have become the scum of the earth, the refuse of the world."

2 Corinthians 1 : 8 - 9.

(8) " We do not want you to be uninformed, brothers, about the hardships

we suffered in the province of Asia. We were under great pressure, far beyond our ability to endure, so that we despaired even of life.

(9) Indeed, in our hearts we felt the sentence of death. But this happened that we might not rely on ourselves but on God, who raises the dead."

2 Timothy 2 : 3

(3) " Endure hardship with us like a good soldier of Christ Jesus."

2 Timothy 2 : 10 - 13

(10) " Therefore I endure everything

for the sake of the elect, that they too may obtain the salvation that is in Christ Jesus, with eternal glory."

(11) Here is a trustworthy saying :
        If we died with him,
            we also live with him;

(12) if we endure,
            we will also reign with him.
        If we disown him,
            he will also disown us;

(13) if we are faithless,
            he will remain faithful,
            for he cannot disown himself."

2 Timothy 4 : 5

(5) " But you, keep your head in all situations, endure hardship, do the work of an evangelist, discharge all duties of your ministry."

Hebrews 12 : 2 - 3.

(2) " Let us fix our eyes on Jesus, the author and perfecter of our faith, who for the joy set before him endured the cross, scorning its shame, and sat down at the right hand of the throne of God.

(3) Consider him who endured such opposition from sinful men, so that you will not grow weary and lose heart."

Hebrews 12 : 7

(7) " Endure hardship as discipline; God is treating you as sons. For what son is not disciplined by his father? "

1 Peter 2 : 20

(20) " But how is it to your credit if you receive a beating for doing wrong and endure it? But if you suffer for doing good and you endure it, this is commendable before God.

(21) To this you were called, because Christ suffered for you, leaving you an example, that you should follow in his steps."

Revelation 2 : 3

(3) You have persevered and have endured hardships for my name, and have not grown weary."

Revelation 3 : 10

(10) " Since you have kept my command to endure patiently, I will also keep you from the hour of trial that is going to come upon the whole world to test those who live on the earth."

{ Heb - Gk Study Bible NIV }

Endures

We now have reached the last I letter of the word ' hope ' and may well be the most important one of the lot. In some ways the word endures, is a summary statement of all that has gone before in this book. There is a clear call and even in our day particularly its a clarion call to endure to the end. The end being the second coming of Jesus Christ, the Son of God and the New earth and heavens. All of which in the end is what the ' hope of glory ' is all about in its fullest sense of its meaning and importance for us all.

We need to endure to the end of the race of our lives and not to give up on our ' hope ', need to overcome and persevere in and through the name of Jesus Christ. We can only hope to ever do this when we trust in His power, authority and strength. We of and in ourselves do not possess the strength or power and even the ability to endure by ourselves. That is why we were made to be ' God - dependent ' rather than to be independent creatures. We need the Creator God to be in and through us and our lives to help us in a very real need and our ' helpless estate'.

In Australia we have trees and various forms of vegetation that endure in the harshest conditions on the planet. Some of them grow in places where with all belief and common sense they should not be able to grow and survive and even prosper. That is the landscape of the red dusty plains and the deserts of the interior of Australia. In some ways it strikes me that this is how the Christian Church and Christians need to and should endure in this world until the return of the rightful King and Lord of the Universe Jesus Christ the Son of God. These plants do not bend or buckle despite the prevailing conditions around them. They survive against all the odds and survive and even prosper in the face of great adversity and in the harshest conditions that the country can throw at them. Sometimes the very creation around us can and does give us an example and teaches us lessons that we should emulate and seek to follow.

EPILOGUE :

The title of this book is Hope , hope, overcomes, perseveres and endures. I have attempted to show how important it is to have a ' hope ', the ' hope of glory' that involves and does all these things. There is a crying need for the Christian Church and even

Christians individually to be the ' beacons of hope ' they were intended to be and even I believe are called to be by both the Word of God and Jesus Christ Himself. ' Hope ' is in short supply in today's world and the world and even we as Christians need to have and evidences our real " hope' , the ' hope of glory '.

Our ' hope ', the ' hope of glory ' is in and through Jesus Christ. I believe the time has come for the Christian Church and Christians at an individual level to stand and be the ' beacons of hope ' they were both always meant to be. The world needs us to be the ' beacons of hope'. They will not get ' hope ' from any other place or from any other avenue or avenues.

Finally, the ' hope of glory ' is I believe ultimately intrinsically tied up with the second coming of Jesus Christ the Son of God. When we preach in our Churches, at times we do not preach the second coming and all that the ' hope of glory ' entails. The Christian church is the one who can offer the world real ' hope ' of a future with Jesus Christ , in and through Him.

At times one can begin
to wonder whether both the
Christian Church and
individual Christians real do
have a real belief and hope
in the second coming of
Jesus Christ? There is now,
with the way and ways of
this world, to stand and
evidence real belief and
' hope ' in the ' hope of
glory'. The second coming of
Jesus Christ, its His gift to us

and through us His gift to a waiting and watching world and its numerous and varied cultures and people groups.

Remember that He wants representatives from every tribe, culture and people groups around His throne of Grace at the end of time.

Amen, Amen and Amen.
Shalom .....

Lightning Source UK Ltd.
Milton Keynes UK
UKHW020646070619

344040UK00009B/188/P